THE THINGS MENTALLY STRONG DO TO BE SUCCESSFUL

The Highly Effective Traits Of Strong Minded People

ERICA CHRIS

INTRODUCTION

You are aware of the link between your mental health and total wellness. Because of this, you should never let your career come before your health and well-being.

How many of these qualities do you possess? There are many qualities that distinguish a strong leader, as well as several illustrations of the non-technical talents that many employers want in today's workers. In order to enhance your job as well as your quest to increase your mental toughness, it is worthwhile to cultivate them.

One of the most important abilities of the twenty-first century is mental toughness, along with emotional intelligence, critical thinking, and information literacy. Due to the enormous amount of information we are exposed to every day, having a healthy mind not only makes one happier but also makes one more productive.

Have you ever questioned how some people are able to maintain their composure in the most trying circumstances while others flip out? They are able to handle challenges because they have honed their mental toughness muscle. And while the majority of people think that mental toughness comes naturally, you can actually practice and improve it just like any other talent.

The discipline to maintain certain behaviors that the majority is striving to avoid is what sets mentally strong people apart from the others. People who are mentally tough are in charge of themselves and their emotions rather than letting life happen to them. Although they are aware that they cannot control life, they do not allow events to influence how they feel or act.

They enjoy other people's successes because they know that those who can't handle it won't ever achieve their own. People with strong mental capacities understand that finding others with similar interests makes life more enjoyable.

But what really sets people with strong minds apart is their capacity to rejoice in the accomplishments of others. People with strong mental faculties don't view others as rivals but rather as allies in their pursuit of achievement.

There is little doubt that working together to achieve success is more enjoyable than dreading rivalry. People who have a strong mental fortitude tend to be social and seek out methods to help others. But surrounding oneself with the appropriate people is the first step. You won't have much to celebrate if the people around you choose binge-watching Netflix than pursuing their aspirations.

However, if you're around individuals who aim high and pursue ambitious projects, you'll find loads of justifications for hosting get-togethers. If we share our successes and setbacks with like-minded individuals, life is much more enjoyable. Stop being afraid of rivalry, and begin assembling a tribe of individuals who will cheer you on as you rise to the top.

Mentally strong people don't criticize themselves even when they are eager for criticism and progress. They consistently engage in self-analysis, yet they don't criticize themselves. Instead, they take a pragmatic approach to extracting as much information as they can from their mistakes.

We are all aware of the significance of effective communication. But we frequently fail to have pleasant conversations with ourselves. Instead, we condemn our behaviors, appearances, and results. Because of this, mentally strong people have positive relationships with their inner critics. They strive for greatness yet resist allowing the inner critic to undermine them. Instead, they are their own biggest supporters and are adept at boosting their spirits and enthusiasm when things are bad. They cultivate an atmosphere that supports their ability to maintain focus and prevent negativity from getting in their way, either directly or indirectly, through others or themselves.

CHAPTER ONE

1. They Control Their Thoughts to Prevent Chaos

A person with a strong mental capacity can manage their thoughts. They keep an eye on their thoughts as they pass rather than allowing them go wild. They are aware that they are not their ideas. Instead, their choices in action shape who they are. People with significant mental faculties will express their opinions about particular acts. They can say to their thoughts, for instance, if they act as if it's the end of the world. They regain more control by identifying the action their thoughts are taking. They develop a stronger mind as a result.

2. They Avoid Attempting to Control Everything

People with strong minds avoid trying to exert total control. They are well aware that there is no way to avoid the fact that life does happen occasionally. Suddenly, loved ones pass away. On occasion, we lose our jobs. Sometimes, ailments overwhelm our state of health. Living in the now is all we can do. While we are here, cherish your loved ones. Take steps to maintain our health while we still have it. Moreover, take charge of what you can. And truly own responsibility for those things. You must let go of the things you can't control and focus on the ones you can in order to become psychologically strong.

3. They Compliment Themselves to Others

Positive self-talk is essential if you want to develop your mental fortitude. Putting oneself down for even the smallest error is over. Never say out loud, "I'm terrible at this," or "I can't do this." You can do anything, even if it takes a little extra patience, since you don't stink. It sometimes helps to be patient with oneself when speaking pleasantly to yourself. You will at times face difficulties. And that's when using constructive self-talk is so crucial. How do you stop your brain from constantly being judgmental and speaking harshly to itself? Avoid being your worst enemy. Become your biggest advocate instead.

4. They Appreciate What They Have

People with strong mental faculties routinely express thanks. Some people keep journals where they list all the things for which they are thankful. Some people make lists of everything they have so they never forget the good things in their lives. Some people might exhibit thankfulness when speaking with others. They might express their gratitude for that person's presence to a friend.

5. They Reflect

Anyone who wants to develop their mental fortitude can do it with some easy meditation.

Even only 10 or 20 minutes a day of practice can help you gain a sense of clarity that will make approaching decisions and conversations much simpler. Your brain may be rewired as a result. According to research, people who frequently meditate have different brains than those who don't. Your mental health can benefit greatly from these changes in the brain. It can do a lot of things, like lowering stress levels and preventing brain illnesses. Some of the advantages of meditation are listed here.

6. They Are Present-Day Residents

Mentally strong people are present-oriented. You could be tempted to replay unpleasant memories in your head or harbor fears about the future. But psychologically strong people emphasize remaining in the present. They are aware of their thoughts when they veer toward the past or the future, but they observe how they pass.

You can concentrate on the experiences taking place in the present by staying in the moment. That is not only a great way to develop mental toughness, but it is also a great way to live. Don't let your thoughts rule your actions. Get out of it and explore the world you are now living in.

7. Seek out the Positive

People with strong minds search for the positive in every circumstance they can ponder, "What can I do today to make tomorrow a little bit better?" during trying circumstances. They move cautiously. But they also keep an eye out for baby highlights. Perhaps you had the worst day of your life today. Perhaps you lost someone who meant the world to you.

Did anything positive occur today? Perhaps it's as simple as having your entire family console you in your grief. Maybe they made an effort to console you with the proper words. It's crucial to find the bright side of challenging circumstances. You grow weaker rather than stronger when you have a "half-empty" perspective on the world.

8. Rewire the Mind

People with strong minds attempt to rewire their brains. Your brain can be altered in a few different ways. It is known as neuroplasticity. You can achieve this by meditating, exercising, reading, listening to music, sleeping, and many other activities. Let's face it, accomplishing this isn't simple. Actually, it's very challenging. If you've ever struggled to quit a habit, keep in mind that the brain is also susceptible to becoming somewhat habituated. It's challenging to tell the brain "no, stop, I want to hear something positive" if you repeatedly think negative thoughts.

9. They Make Fun of Themselves

Occasionally, things utterly fail. The one thing mentally strong individuals do differently though, is laugh at themselves rather than criticize them.

We all err from time to time. Being rejected is common. Humans are imperfect by nature. And mentally strong people overcome by letting go of all the anguish and finding delight in being wholly defective. When things don't go your way, laughter can help you get mentally strong by lifting you back up.

10. They Take Care of Themselves

Self-care is something that daily self-reliant people do. They are some of the strongest people ever because of all the little things they do every day. It might be as easy as dancing their negativity away or having a good lunch every day.

Simple routines like taking a eucalyptus-scented shower or using soap with a lavender aroma will help lessen those daily tensions. You might be surprised to learn that persons with great mental health typically engage in a variety of short-term self-care activities each day that they can easily include into their daily routine. Because, let's face it, nobody on earth is going to take care of you if you don't practice self-care. It is entirely up to you to express that type of love to yourself.

11. They Set Goals

You must establish goals for yourself if you want to become mentally powerful. The ones that break apart most frequently are those who don't set goals they wish to achieve. You should have a daily goal. You'll make sacrifices that no one else would if you are clear on whom you want to be, what you want to achieve, and the impact you want to have on the world. You develop a strong mentality through persistence, motivation, and determination. Setting goals can help you focus intensely. When you are clear about what you want from life, you are less likely to give up when a tiny hurdle gets in your way. You only leap.

12. They Sleep Enough

It's challenging to exaggerate how crucial sleep is to developing mental resilience. Toxic proteins that are by-products of neural activity while you're awake are eliminated by your brain when you sleep. Unfortunately, your brain can only effectively remove them while you sleep, so if you don't get enough sleep, the toxic proteins stay in your brain cells and disrupt your thinking, causing problems that no amount of caffeine can reverse.

Mentally tough people prioritize getting great sleep because they are aware that when they don't receive enough or the correct kind of sleep, their ability to maintain self-control, focus, and memory is all negatively impacted.

They also make sure to get their recommended eight hours of sleep each night. They are completely aware that their mind requires regular sleep in order to function at its optimum. They do not exert excessive effort on themselves. They don't stay up late working to complete a project or catch up on work. People with strong mental faculties are aware of the necessity of sleep for optimal performance. They are aware of the necessity of sleep for maintaining emotional control. They are aware of the necessity of sleep in order to meet life's obstacles. Therefore, sleep isn't for the weak if you want to put yourself in the best frame of mind possible. It is for the powerful.

Having difficulty going to sleep at night? Try one of our sleep meditation routines that we offer for free. By calming your body and clearing your mind of distractions, it will assist you in setting the proper circumstances for sleep.

14. They Eat Healthily

You must feed your body well if you want to become mentally powerful. Of course, you are allowed to occasionally satisfy your sweet taste. However, those who are intellectually strong also eat a nutritious diet, including fruits, vegetables, and whole grains. They consume healthy meals since they are aware that this is how they obtain their vitamins and nutrients. And those nutrients maintain their bodily and mental wellbeing.

You might feel groggier or more irritable when you're deficient in nutrients or vitamins and not understand why.

15. They Don't Frequently Use Social Media

Social networking is rarely used by those with powerful minds. They limit their social media use rather than engaging in comparison games on Instagram or the grass is greener effect. Perhaps they only follow accounts that make them feel better or happier. Or, to improve their mental health, they occasionally engage in a social media detox.

Avoid falling into the politics, click bait, and comparison negative spiral that dominates most social media if you want to develop a strong mind. But if you're unable to break your social media addiction, keep in mind to select accounts to follow that inspire you. If you look closely enough, you can find them.

16. They Read Books

People with powerful minds enjoy reading. They read enchanting books to learn or amuse themselves instead of binge-watching mind-numbing shows on Netflix for hours. Check out our list of recommended meditation books if you're interested in learning more.

And while reading non-fiction books might teach you a lot, reading fiction novels occasionally is quite good. By creating imaginary worlds in your imagination as you read, it can help you develop your creativity. Reading is magical because it gives you fresh insights. Other individuals have a lot to teach you. And you can enhance yourself by developing your communication skills, your mental fortitude, or your character. You improve as you get more knowledge from others. Open a good book, and then open your mind.

17. They Anticipate Changes

People with high mental faculties are adaptable. They are aware that they can't fight it. Whether they like it or not, they know it will happen. Change will always occur. There will be breakdowns followed by creative re-assemblies. When anything changes, consider it a fresh chance and experience. You will be less happy the more you fight it. But if you approach experiences, even the difficult ones, as learning opportunities, you'll be on the proper path to developing a strong mind.

CHAPTER TWO

1. A Few Essential Behaviors Of Mentally Strong People

a. They Have Emotional Intelligence

The foundation of mental toughness is emotional intelligence. Without the capacity to completely comprehend, accept, and act upon intensely negative feelings, you cannot be mentally tough. Moments that put your mental fortitude to the test ultimately put your emotional IQ to the test (EQ).

Your EQ is a variable skill that you can develop with knowledge and effort, unlike your IQ, which is fixed. It makes sense that persons with high EQs make $28,000 more a year (on average) than those with low EQs and that 90% of top performers have high EQs.

b. They Have Self-Belief

You are correct whether you believe you can or cannot. Mentally tough people agree with

Ford's assertion that your mindset has a significant impact on your capacity for success. This idea is true; it's not merely a motivating idea. According to a recent University of Melbourne study, those who are more confident tend to earn greater salaries and advance through the ranks more swiftly than others.

True confidence has a distinctive appearance as contrasted to the phony confidence people display to hide their fears. Mentally tough individuals have an advantage over the sceptical and dubious because their self-assurance motivates others and enables them to effect change.

c. They Remove Toxic Individuals

Most people find it irritating and exhausting to deal with tough people. Mentally tough individuals manage their dealings with poisonous individuals by maintaining emotional restraint. They use a logical approach when they have to deal with a poisonous person. They are aware of their feelings and resist letting resentment or rage contribute to the commotion. They are able to find points of agreement and resolve issues by taking into account the challenging person's perspective.

Mentally tough people are able to handle the poisonous person with a grain of salt even when everything fully goes wrong so they don't let them drag them down.

d. They Accept Change.

People that are mentally tough are adaptable and flexible. They are aware that their prosperity and happiness are seriously jeopardized by their paralyzing dread of change. They keep an eye out for impending change and create a plan of action in the event that it does. You can only see the positive aspects of change when you embrace it.

If you want to notice and seize the chances that change creates, you must do so with an open heart and mind. When you continue to act in the same manner, hoping that the absence of change will make it go away, you are doomed to failure. After all, doing the same thing repeatedly and expecting a different outcome is the definition of insanity.

e. They Oppose

According to research done at the University of California, San Francisco, it is more difficult to say no, which increases your risk of experiencing stress, burnout, and even depression. Saying no is healthy, and mentally tough people have the confidence and foresight to be unambiguous about it.

Mentally tough people refrain from using expressions like "I don't believe I can" or "I'm not sure" when it's time to say no. They refuse new commitments with confidence because they are aware that doing so respects their current obligations and offers them the chance to successfully carry them out.

Additionally, mentally tough people are able to exercise self-control by telling themselves no. They postpone satisfaction and refrain from harmful impulsive behavior.

F. They Are Aware That Regret Is Primarily Caused By Fear.

Mentally tough people are aware that, in the end, they will regret their missed opportunities much more than their failures. Don't be hesitant to take chances.

People frequently ask, "What could possibly go wrong for you? Will you die from it? The worst thing that can happen to you is not necessarily death. The worst thing you can do is allow yourself to pass away internally while you're still alive.

To walk this narrow line between dwelling and remembering, one must have sophisticated self-awareness. You get nervous and fearful if you dwell on your mistakes for too long, and you are forced to repeat them if you entirely forget about them.

Your capacity to turn setbacks into opportunities for growth is the secret to maintaining equilibrium. Because of this, you have a tendency to get back up quickly after falling.

g. They Accept Failure.

People with a strong mentality welcome failure because they understand that it is the foundation for success. Nobody has ever achieved true success without first learning to accept defeat.

Your errors help you succeed by pointing out when you're taking the incorrect way. Usually, when you're feeling the most stuck and frustrated, the largest breakthroughs occur. This frustration pushes you to rethink your approach, think creatively, and see the answer you've been missing.

h. They Avoid Focusing on Mistakes.

People with strong mental faculties are aware that your emotional state depends on where you focus your attention. Fixating on your problems causes tension and bad emotions to build up over time, which impairs performance. When you concentrate on taking steps to improve your situation and yourself, you develop a sense of personal efficacy, which fosters good feelings and enhances performance.

People with strong mental faculties put their mistakes behind them but don't forget them.

They are able to adapt and make adjustments for success in the future by storing their blunders at a safe distance yet still accessible to refer to.

i. They Won't Allow Anyone to Stem Their Joy

You are no longer in control of your own happiness when your sense of pleasure and satisfaction comes from evaluating yourself in relation to other people. When psychologically tough people feel good about what they do, they won't let other people's judgments or achievements diminish that feeling.

You may always take other people's opinions with a grain of salt; even if it's impossible to stop your reactions to what other people think of you. You also don't have to compare yourself to others.

Mentally tough people are aware that they are never as good or horrible as other people claim they are, regardless of what others may be thinking of them at any one time.

j. And They Don't Restrict Other People's Joy.

Because they understand that everyone has something to contribute and that they don't need to diminish others in order to feel good about themselves, mentally tough people don't judge others.

It is limiting to evaluate oneself in relation to others. You lose all energy to jealousy and anger because they are such powerful energy drainers. People with a strong mentality don't waste time or effort evaluating others and fretting about how they compare.

Put your efforts into gratitude rather than squandering it on jealousy. You both gain when you acknowledge others' achievements.

k. They Workout

People who exercised twice a week for 10 weeks felt more socially, academically, and athletically competent, according to a research from the Eastern Ontario Research Institute. They gave themselves higher marks for self-esteem and body image. Best of all, the instantaneous, endorphin-fueled happiness from exercise made all the difference instead of the physical changes in their bodies being to blame for the rise in confidence, which is essential to mental toughness.

People with strong minds often work out. They are able to effectively release all of the tension or stress from their bodies thanks to the physical activity. Running, dancing, or engaging in other cardio or strength training routines allow you to let all the tension out rather than holding it in. People with great mental faculties do so because they manage their anger in constructive ways. When people hold their stress inside, they finally blow up and release it all at once.

But if you routinely relieve any physical stress, you'll be more prepared to express your grievances in a constructive way. Resulting in the exact solution you seek.

1. They Consume Caffeine in Moderation

Excessive coffee consumption causes the adrenaline, which is the root of the fight-or-flight response, to be released. The fight-or-flight response forgoes reason in favor of a quicker action to protect survival. This is excellent when a bear is after you, but it is less advantageous when life presents a challenge.

Your emotions take control of your conduct when caffeine puts your brain and body into this hyper-aroused state of tension. Given that caffeine takes its sweet time to leave your body, its lengthy half-life assures that you stay in this state. People with strong minds are aware that drinking too much coffee might be harmful, yet they do not let it affect them.

m. They Forgive Without Waiting for an Apology.

Mentally resilient individuals are aware that letting go of grudges and forgiving those who have never apologized makes life much easier. Grudges allow unpleasant memories from your past to sour your delight today. The emotional parasites that sabotage your delight in life are hatred and anger.

Hanging onto tension can have disastrous effects since it causes your body to experience bad emotions that come with holding onto a grudge (both physically and mentally). When you forgive someone, you are not endorsing what they did; rather, you are releasing yourself from being their victim for all time.

n. They're Unwaveringly Positive

If you pay attention to the news for any length of time, you'll see that it's just a never-ending cycle of violent attacks, war, weak economy, failed businesses, and environmental catastrophes. It's simple to believe that everything is going bad very quickly.

Who knows, though? Perhaps it is. But because they don't get bogged down in things outside of their control, mentally tough people don't worry about it. They concentrate their energies on focusing their attention and effort on the two things that are entirely under their control rather than trying to create a revolution overnight.

CHAPTER THREE

Conclusion

People with powerful minds avoid trying to manipulate their surroundings. They make fun of themselves, create goals, look after their health, show gratitude, and engage in so many other admirable behaviors. They don't have good fortune and only experience positive things. Instead, they find the positive in challenging circumstances. While they face difficulties just like everyone else does, they take care of themselves and let go of things they can't control in order to put themselves in the best possible situation. Not everyone is born with the ability to be mentally tough. It is achievable and enjoyable.

Building mental toughness is closely related to building physical toughness. Numerous studies have shown that our physical and mental health is correlated. The more physically fit you are, the sharper your mind will be, therefore mentally tough people take good care of their sleep habits, as well as their nutrition and frequent exercise to keep in shape. In the short run, it may be effective to put your health at risk in order to do more, but in the long run, it will undoubtedly backfire.

High achievers put time, money, and energy into improving both their physical and mental health. They also take as much care of their bodies as they do of their mental health.

A sound body guarantees a secure mind, which again guarantees wise decisions and even more healthy options. You'll quickly discover yourself in a cycle of beneficial effects that not only affect your body but also your mind once you've managed to make every day, small changes that are good for your health.

They are aware that change is a constant in life and that nothing ever remains the same for an extended period of time. As a result, they always look for difficulties and novel circumstances as opposed to remaining in their comfort zones. By exposing themselves to uncharted territory, individuals develop their capacity for adaptation and ensure that they are fast to react to novel circumstances.

Mentally strong people constantly strive for advancement, in contrast to mentally weak persons who are terrified of change. In addition to accepting change, they actively look for fresh obstacles and development possibilities. Mentally tough people, as opposed to weak ones, have confidence in their capacity to overcome obstacles. It's normal to be overwhelmed by abrupt changes, yet every shift also presents an opportunity for growth and new prospects. Mentally strong people accept change rather than resisting it and have faith in their capacity to adapt and get beyond any challenges.

www.ingramcontent.com/pod-product-compliance
Lightning Source LLC
LaVergne TN
LVHW052109160826
845678LV00015B/3451